DATE DUE

17622
96-

	E 978.004 PEN		Penner, Lucille Recht. Sitting bull	
JY 16 '96				
NO 5 '96				
JE 24 '97				
AG 23 '97				
OC 22 '98				
MY 27 '99				

DEMCO 25-370

Put Beginning Readers on the Right Track with
ALL ABOARD READING™

The All Aboard Reading series is especially for beginning readers. Written by noted authors and illustrated in full color, these are books that children really and truly *want* to read—books to excite their imagination, tickle their funny bone, expand their interests, and support their feelings. With three different reading levels, All Aboard Reading lets you choose which books are most appropriate for your children and their growing abilities.

Level 1—for Preschool through First Grade Children
Level 1 books have very few lines per page, very large type, easy words, lots of repetition, and pictures with visual "cues" to help children figure out the words on the page.

Level 2—for First Grade to Third Grade Children
Level 2 books are printed in slightly smaller type than Level 1 books. The stories are more complex, but there is still lots of repetition in the text and many pictures. The sentences are quite simple and are broken up into short lines to make reading easier.

Level 3—for Second Grade through Third Grade Children
Level 3 books have considerably longer texts, use harder words and more complicated sentences.

All Aboard for happy reading!

To Alex, Patrick, and Eleanor Beilby
—Lucy

To Kyle with love—Uncle Will

Special thanks to Ray Winters of the Hunkpapa
and Santee Dakota nation for helping to make this book
as accurate as possible.

Text copyright © 1995 by Lucille Recht Penner. Illustrations copyright © 1995 by Wood
Ronsaville Harlin. All rights reserved. Published by Grosset & Dunlap, Inc., which is a member
of The Putnam & Grosset Group, New York. ALL ABOARD READING is a trademark of The
Putnam & Grosset Group. GROSSET & DUNLAP is a trademark of Grosset & Dunlap, Inc.
Published simultaneously in Canada. Printed in the U.S.A.

Library of Congress Cataloging-in-Publication Data

Penner, Lucille Recht.
    Sitting Bull / by Lucille Recht Penner ; illustrated by Will Williams.
        p.   cm. — (All aboard reading)
    "Level 2, grades 1–3."
    1. Sitting Bull, 1834?–1890—Juvenile literature.   2. Dakota Indians—Biography—Juvenile
literature.   3. Sitting Bull, 1834?–1890.   [1. Dakota Indians—Biography.   2. Indians of
North America—Biography.]   I. Williams, Will, ill.   II. Title.   III. Series.
E99.D1S6128   1995
978.004′975′0092—dc20
    [B]   94-46766
                                                                                                                        CIP
ISBN 0-448-40938-0 (GB)   A B C D E F G H I J   AC

ISBN 0-448-40937-2 (pbk)   A B C D E F G H I J

ALL
ABOARD
READING™

Level 2
Grades 1-3

Sitting Bull

By Lucille Recht Penner
Illustrated by Will Williams

Grosset & Dunlap • New York

4

Who was the greatest Indian chief of all?

Many people say it was Sitting Bull.

Sitting Bull was a Hunkpapa.

(You say it like this: HUNK-pa-pa.)

His tribe lived on

the Great Northern Plains,

where they hunted buffalo.

When Sitting Bull was a boy,

everyone called him Slow.

It was the right name for him.

He ate slowly.

He moved slowly.

He even talked slowly.

But he was watching
and learning all the time.

When Slow was only ten years old,

he killed his first buffalo.

Now he was a hunter.

But more than anything,

Slow wanted to be a great warrior.

One day, the Hunkpapas

went to fight against the Crow.

Slow was only a boy,

but he jumped on his pony

and galloped after the men.

Slow had no weapons.

No bow.

No arrows.

All he had was a long red stick.

It was called a coup stick.

(You say it like this: COO.)

But that was all he needed.

Striking an enemy with a coup stick
was the bravest thing a warrior could do.
When the men came near the Crow,
Slow raced ahead of everyone else.

A Crow warrior saw Slow coming.

The Crow raised his bow and arrow

to shoot.

But Slow was quick!

He hit the warrior with the coup stick,

knocked the bow out of his hands,

and galloped away.

That night the Hunkpapas
sat together under the stars.
"Now," Slow's father said to his son,
"you are a warrior!"
He gave Slow a new name,
a name full of power—
Sitting Bull.

Soon there were many stories

about Sitting Bull.

One day, he lay down under a tree.

Above him a bird tapped on a branch.

It seemed to tap a message:

Stay still!

Suddenly a grizzly bear stood over him.

It was so close

he could smell its hot breath.

But he stayed very still

until the grizzly lumbered off.

Sitting Bull thanked the bird.

He said, "The bird people

will be my friends forever."

Once, the warriors

fought some of their enemies.

Only a little boy was left alive.

The boy cried, "Help me!"

Sitting Bull was sorry for him.

"Let him live," Sitting Bull said.

"I will treat him like a brother."

And he did.

After a battle, Sitting Bull

never rode away—

not until everyone else was safe.

No wonder his people

made him their chief.

But trouble was coming.

White settlers moved

onto Hunkpapa land.

They built roads,

towns, and forts.

Soldiers came too.

The soldiers tried to make
the Indians leave their homes.
They wanted the Indians to live
on pieces of land called reservations.

They would not be free

to follow the buffalo.

Many tribes didn't want to live

on the reservations.

They decided to fight together

under one chief.

They chose Sitting Bull to be their leader.

They gave him a great war bonnet

of eagle feathers,

and a beautiful white horse.

More and more soldiers came.

But the Indians fought hard for their land.

In one battle

the soldiers killed many warriors.

Sitting Bull said,

"We must turn back."

Some warriors said no.

They said, "Only cowards turn back."

"I am not a coward,"

Sitting Bull told them.

He walked toward the soldiers.

Bullets were flying around him.

Sitting Bull sat down

and smoked his pipe.

No one ever called him

a coward again.

In 1876, a famous soldier named

George Custer said,

"Indians don't know how to fight.

I will whip them."

But he was wrong.

One day Custer attacked

a village of Hunkpapas.

They were camped

beside the Little Bighorn river.

Warriors killed Custer

and all his men.

Soon everyone in America heard about

the Battle of the Little Bighorn.

More soldiers came.

They were angry.

They wanted revenge.

They chased Sitting Bull and his people.

The Indians couldn't hunt or rest.

They were always hungry and tired.

Sitting Bull led his people

north to Canada.

It was safe there.

U.S. soldiers couldn't follow them.

But the weather was cold.

There were few buffalo.

The people were very sad.

They missed their home.

So Sitting Bull led them back.

Sitting Bull knew the time

for fighting was over.

He went to live on a reservation.

Soldiers gave him a hoe.

They told him,

"Grow your own food."

Sitting Bull was a hunter.

He was not a farmer.

But he did what they said.

Then a man came to visit him.

His name was Buffalo Bill Cody.

He said Sitting Bull was famous.

People would pay to see him.

So Sitting Bull joined Buffalo Bill's

Great Wild West Show!

There were sharpshooters,

dancing girls, cowboys,

and rodeo riders.

Many people came to see

the great chief.

Some booed.

Some cheered.

They paid money for his autograph.

Sitting Bull gave the money away

to beggar boys who followed the show.

Sitting Bull went back to the reservation.

His place was with his people.

He was growing old.

And he was tired.

But the soldiers were still afraid of him.

Was he going to lead the Indians
against them once more?
They made a plan.
Indians who worked for the soldiers
would arrest Sitting Bull.

The men sneaked into
Sitting Bull's cabin at dawn.
They pulled the old chief
out of bed.

Friends ran to help him.

There was shouting and pushing.

Suddenly a shot rang out.

Sitting Bull fell to the ground— dead.

The news spread over the land

that once belonged to the Indians.

Sitting Bull was gone.

But he would be remembered—

always.